GEORGE SEFERIS
POEMS

George Seferis

POEMS

TRANSLATED FROM THE
GREEK BY

Rex Warner

An Atlantic Monthly Press Book

LITTLE, BROWN AND COMPANY

Boston   *Toronto*

Third Printing

ATLANTIC–LITTLE, BROWN BOOKS
ARE PUBLISHED BY
LITTLE, BROWN AND COMPANY
IN ASSOCIATION WITH
THE ATLANTIC MONTHLY PRESS

PRINTED IN THE UNITED STATES OF AMERICA

Foreword

In making the translation of these poems I have been aided, in the first place, by the poet himself, who has most generously given me very much of his time and of his attention. I cannot thank him sufficiently for his kindness, his patience, and also for the great pleasure which I have found in our work and in our conversations.

I would wish also to express my deep gratitude to our friend, George Savidis, who has made versions of many of the poems, adhering most strictly to the text, and allowed me to use these as the basis for my own work. His help and his criticism have been quite invaluable to me.

I am grateful too to another friend, George Katsimbalis, who, about fifteen years ago, first introduced me to the poetry of Seferis, who encouraged and helped me in my first ambitious venture of translating 'The Thrush', and with whom I have collaborated in the translation both of 'Helen' and of 'Salamis in Cyprus'.

Indeed I have had all the help, and the best help, that anyone could ask for. And still the work, though very enjoyable, has been difficult.

It is always, of course, difficult (some would say impossible) to translate poetry from one language into another. But additional difficulties will confront anyone who attempts to translate modern Greek poetry into modern English. A Greek poet can use a word that is stamped with modernity and put next to it a word straight from Homer or from Byzantium or from the Cretan poets of the seventeenth century. The language, in fact, and the civilisation have a much longer tradition than our own. And Seferis, eminent as he is as a European poet, is pre-eminently a Greek poet, conscious of that Greek tradition which shaped, and indeed created, the tradition of Europe, but which, in very modern as in very ancient times, has often developed differently. Throughout the poetry of Seferis one will notice his profound consciousness of the presence of the past, and of its weight. There is also to be observed an extraordinary freshness of vision. Objects, recognised and felt to be extremely old, are seen suddenly, as for the first time.

But here I do not wish to attempt any kind of criticism or explanation. My aim is only to stress some of the differences—of language, of tradition and of experience—which make the translation of these particular poems difficult.

There are also difficulties which may be described as technical. Once Seferis said to me 'If I had to have a kind of motto for my poetry, I suppose it would be something like "In my poverty is my strength" '. Not that there is any 'poverty' in the language; but he will never use two words where one is sufficient, and each word has its weight, its colour or what he calls its 'halo'. Superficially it may appear that this kind of strong poverty should be a help to the translator, and indeed it is sometimes possible to translate word for word. Yet if one goes rather more deeply into the matter one will find that it may be more difficult to translate a word than a sentence. The work becomes a particularly delicate work of precision. And of course one is never satisfied with the result.

Some of these poems have already appeared in England in translations by Bernard Spencer, Nanos Valaoritis and Lawrence Durrell under the title of 'The King of Asine', published by John Lehmann in 1948. I have no wish to attempt to supersede these excellent translations. But, in a volume which, like this one, is longer and which attempts to give a rather more complete idea of the poet's work, it seemed desirable that all the translations should be by the same hand.

Rex Warner

Contents

I

MYTHISTOREMA

'Si j'ai du goût, ce n'est guères
Que pour la terre et les pierres.'

Arthur Rimbaud

I

The messenger,
Three years we waited for him eagerly;
We kept looking very closely at
The shore the pines the stars.
Joining the blade of the plough or the ship's keel
We were searching to find again the first seed
So that the immemorial drama might begin once more.

We came back to our homes broken,
Weak in the limb, mouths ravaged
From taste of the rust and of the brine.
When we awoke we travelled northwards, strangers,
Plunged into mists by immaculate wings of swans
Which wounded us.
In the winter nights the strong wind from the east maddened us.
In the summer we were lost in the agony of the day that would not die.
We brought back
These carvings of a humble art.

II

Again another well inside a cave.
Once it was easy
To bring up from its depth idols and ornaments
To give pleasure to the friends who still remained faithful to us.

The ropes have broken now; only their marks on the well's mouth
Remind us of our departed happiness:
The fingers on the rim, as the poet says.
The fingers feel for a moment the cool of the stone
And the body's fever passes into the stone
And the cave stakes its soul and loses it
Every second, full of silence, without a drop.

III

Remember the baths where you were slain

I awoke with this marble head between my hands
Which tires my elbows out. Where can I put it down?
It was falling into the dream as I rose from the dream
And so our lives grew one, hard now to be separated.

I peer into the eyes, neither shut nor open,
I speak to the mouth which is always trying to speak,
I hold the cheeks which have grown beyond the skin.
I can do no more.

My hands are lost, my hands come back to me,
Maimed.

IV

Argonauts

And for the soul
If it is to know itself
It is into a soul
That it must look.
The stranger and the enemy, we have seen him in the mirror.

They were good lads, the comrades. They did not grumble
Because of weariness or because of thirst or because of frost.
They had the manner of trees and the manner of waves
That accept the wind and the rain,
Accept the night and the sun,
And in the midst of change they do not change.
They were good lads. Day after day with downcast eyes
They used to sweat at the oar,
Breathing rhythmically,
And their blood flushed up to an obedient skin.
There was a time when they sang, with downcast eyes,
When we passed the desert island with the Arabian figs,
Towards the setting of the sun, beyond the cape
Of dogs that howl.
If it is to know itself, they used to say,
It is into a soul it must look, they used to say.
And the oars beat on the gold of the sea
In the middle of sunset.
Many the capes we passed, many the islands, the sea

Which brings the other sea, sea-gulls and seals.
There were times when unfortunate women with lamentations
Cried out for their children gone,
And others with wild faces looked for Great-Alexander
And glories sunken in the depths of Asia.
We anchored by shores steeped in nocturnal perfumes
Among the singing of birds, waters that left on the hands
The recollection of a great good fortune.
But there was never an end to the journeys.
Their souls became one with the oars and the rowlocks,
With the severe figurehead at the prow,
With the wake of the rudder,
With the water that fractured the image of their faces.
One after another the comrades died
With downcast eyes. Their oars
Indicate the places where they sleep on the shore.

There is none to remember them, and the word is Justice.

V

We never knew them.
                    Deep down within us it was hope that said
We had known them ever since childhood.
We saw them twice perhaps; then they took to their ships;
Cargoes of coal, cargoes of grain, and our friends
Lost on the other side of the ocean for ever.
Dawn finds us by the tired lamp
Drawing clumsily and with difficulty on a piece of paper
Boats, figure-heads and shells.
In the evening we go down to the river
Because it shows us the way to the sea
And we pass the nights in cellars that smell of tar.

Our friends have gone
                      perhaps we never saw them, perhaps
We only met them at the time sleep still
Was leading us close up to the breathing wave.
Perhaps we look for them because we are looking for
The other life that is beyond the statues.

VI

M.R.

The garden with its fountains in the rain
You will only see it looking through the low window
Behind the blurred pane of glass. Your room
Will have no light but the fire-light on the hearth
And sometimes in flashes of distant lightning will stand out
The wrinkles on your forehead, my old Friend.

The garden with its fountains which were, in your hands,
A rhythm of the other life, beyond the broken
Marbles and the tragic columns
And a dance among the oleanders
Near the new quarries,
A misted glass will have cut it from your hours.
You will not breathe; the earth and the sap of the trees
Will rush from your memory to beat upon
This pane of glass beaten upon by the rain
From the world outside.

VII

South Wind

The sea to westward joins a trail of mountains.
On our left the south wind blows and drives us mad,
This wind that bares bone, stripping off the flesh.
Our house among the pines and the carobs.
Big windows. Big tables
For writing the letters we have been writing to you
For all these months, and drop
Into the parting between us to fill it up.

Star of morning, when you lowered your eyes
Our times and seasons were more sweet than oil
Laid on a wound, more joyful than the coolness
Of water on the palate, calmer than swan's down.
You held our life in the hollow of your hand.
After the bitter bread of exile,
In the night if we stand by the white wall
Your voice comes to us like the hope of a warming fire;
And once again this wind
Stropping its razor's edge upon our nerves.

Each of us writes to you the same things
And each of us in front of another is silent,
Looking, each one of us apart, at the same world,
The light and the shadow on the trail of mountains
And at you.
Who will lift this sorrow from our hearts?

Yesterday evening came a heavy rain. Today
Again the covered sky. Our thoughts
Like the pine needles after yesterday's rain
Against our door heaped up and useless
Attempt to build a tower which collapses.

Among these decimated villages
Upon this headland naked to the south wind
With the trail of mountains before us, hiding you,
Who will reckon up our decision to forget?
Who will accept our offering at this end of autumn?

VIII

But what are they looking for, our souls that travel
On decks of ships out-worn, crowded together with
Sallow-faced women, crying babies,
Unable to distract themselves even with the flying fish
Or with the stars to which the mast heads point;
Rubbed-out by the gramophone records,
Involved unwillingly in aimless pilgrimages,
Murmuring broken thoughts from foreign languages?

What then are they looking for, our souls that travel
On rotting sea-timbers
From one harbour to another harbour?

Shifting broken stones, breathing in
Each day less easily the pine trees' coolness,
Swimming now in the waters of this sea
And now of that one,
Without the sense of touch,
Without men,
In a country that is no longer our own country
And is not yours either.

We knew it, that the islands were beautiful
Somewhere round about here where we are groping,
Maybe a little lower or a little higher,
No distance away at all.

IX

The harbour is old, I cannot wait any longer
Either for the friend who left for the island of pines
Or for the friend who left for the island of planes
Or for the friend who left for the open sea.

I stroke the rusty cannons, I stroke the oars
So that my body may revive and make its decision.
The sails give out only the smell
Of the salt spray of the other storm.

If I wished to stay by myself, I desired to find
Solitude, I did not desire such endless waiting,
The scattering of my soul to the horizon,
These lines, these colours, this silence.

The stars of night bring me back to the expectation
Of Odysseus for the dead among the asphodels.
Among the asphodels when we moored here we wished to find
The mountain glade that saw Adonis wounded.

X

Our country is a shut-in place, all mountains
And the mountains roofed by a low sky, day and night.
We have no rivers, we have no wells, we have no fountains,
Only some cisterns, empty; they ring and are to us
Objects of worship.
A sound stagnant, hollow, like our solitude,
Like our love and like our bodies.
It seems to us strange that once we were able to build
These houses of ours, these huts, these sheep-folds.
And our marriages,—the dewy garlands, the marriage fingers,
Have become insoluble riddles for our souls.
How were they born
Our children? How then did they grow up?

Our country is a shut-in place. It is enclosed
By the two black Clashing Rocks. And when we go
On Sundays down to the harbour for a breath of air,
We see, lit by the sunset,
The broken timbers of unfinished journeys,
Bodies that know no longer how to love.

XI

Your blood froze sometimes like the moon.
In the inexhaustible night your blood
Spread its white wings above
The black rocks, the shapes of trees and the houses
With a gleam of light out of the years of our childhood.

XII

A bottle in the sea

Three rocks, a few burnt pines, a desert chapel,
And higher up
The same landscape, recopied, begins again.
Three rocks in the form of a gate, rusted,
A few burnt pines black and yellow
And a small square building buried in whitewash;
And up the hill again, over and over,
Just the same landscape climbs in tier after tier
Up to the skyline, up to the sunset sky.

Here we moored our ship to mend our broken oars
To drink some water and to get some sleep.
The sea which embittered us is deep and unexplored,
Unfolding boundless calm.
Here among the shingle we found a coin
And threw dice for it.
The youngest of us won it and disappeared.

We embarked again with our broken oars.

XIII

Hydra

Dolphins banners and cannonades.
The sea that was once so bitter to your soul
Carried the many-coloured and shining ships,
It swayed and rocked them, all blue with white wings,
The sea that was once so bitter to your soul
Now bursting out with colours in the sun.

White sails, light, and the wet oars
With drum-beat rhythm on tamed waves.

Your eyes would be beautiful if they were looking,
Your arms would be splendid if you were stretching them out,
Your lips, as once they were, would come alive
At such a miracle;
You were looking for it what were you looking for in front of the ashes
Or in the rain in the fog in the wind,
Even at the hour when the lights were slackening,
When the city was sinking and from the pavements
The Nazarene showed you his heart,
What were you looking for? Why don't you come? What were you
  looking for?

XIV

Three red doves in the light
Drawing our fate in the light
With colours and gestures of people
Whom we loved.

XV

Quid πλατανῶν opacissimus?

Sleep wrapped you round, like a tree, with green leaves,
You breathing, like a tree in the peaceful light,
And in the limpid pool I looked at your face:
Shut eyelids and the eyelashes brushed the water.
My fingers in the soft grass found your fingers,
I held your pulse for a moment
And felt in another place the pain of your heart.

Under the plane, by the water, among the laurels
Sleep kept displacing and dispersing you
Around me, near me. I could not touch the whole of you
Together with your silence;
Seeing your shadow growing now larger now smaller,
Losing itself in the other shadows, in the other
World which let go of and kept hold of you.

The life which was given to us to live, we lived it.
Pity those who are waiting with such patience
Lost in the black laurels, under the heavy planes,
And those who, solitary, speak to the cisterns and wells
And are drowned within the circles of their voice.
Pity the comrade who shared in our privation and our sweat
And sunk into the sun, like a crow beyond the ruins,
Without a hope of enjoying our reward.

Grant us, outside of sleep, serenity.

XVI

The name—Orestes

Again, again into the track, once more into the track!
How many turns, how many laps of blood, how many black
Circles of faces watching: the people watching me
Who watched me when, upright in the chariot,
I raised my hand, brilliant, and they roared applause.

The froth of horses beats upon my flesh. When will the horses
Weary? The axle shrieks, the axle glows. When will the axle
Seize up in flame? When will the rein break?
When will the whole hooves tread
Full on the ground, on the soft grass, among
The poppies where in spring you picked a daisy?

They were lovely, your eyes. You did not know where to look with them
Nor did I know where to look, I, without a country,
I who struggle on this spot—how many turns and laps!—
And I feel my knees failing me above the axle,
Above the wheels, above the savage track.
The knees fail easily when the gods will have it so.
No one is able to escape; no strength will do it, you cannot
Escape the sea which cradled you, for which you turn and search
In this moment of contest, among the breathing of horses,
With the reeds that used to sing in autumn to a Lydian mode,
The sea that you cannot find again, run as you may,
Turn as you may, lap after lap, in front of the black
Eumenides who are bored and cannot forgive.

XVII

Astyanax

Now that you are going, take with you the child
Who saw the light under that plane tree
On a day when trumpets sounded and armour gleamed
And sweating horses bowed their heads at the trough
Over the green surface, brushing
The water with their moist nostrils.

The olive trees with the wrinkles of our fathers
The rocks with the wisdom of our fathers
And our brother's blood living upon the earth
Were a robust joy a rich injunction
For the souls who understood their prayer.

Now that you are going, now at the dawn of the day
Of final settlement, now that no one can tell
Whom he will kill and how he will meet his end,
Take with you the child who saw the light
Under the leaves of that plane
And teach him to study the trees.

XVIII

I am sorry to have allowed a broad river to pass between my fingers
Without drinking a single drop.
Now I sink into the stone.
A small pine on the red soil
Is all the companionship I have.
What I loved has disappeared with the houses
Which were new last summer
And fell to pieces before the autumn wind.

XIX

Even if the wind blows it bring us no refreshment
And the shadow remains narrow beneath the cypresses
And all around the slopes go up to the mountains.

They weigh heavily on us
The friends who no longer know the way to die.

XX

Andromeda

In my breast the wound opens again
When the stars are setting and become conjoined with my body
When silence falls after the footsteps of men.

These stones which are sinking into the years, how far will they
       drag me with them?
The sea, the sea, who is it that can drain it dry?
I see the hands each dawn beckoning to the hawk and vulture,
I, bound to the rock which suffering has made my own,
I see the trees which breathe the black peace of the dead
And then the smiles, motionless, of the statues.

XXI

We who set out upon this pilgrimage
Looked at the broken statues
We forgot ourselves and said that life
Is not so easily annihilated;
That death has ways that are uncharted
And a justice that is its own;

That while we are dying upright on our feet,
Made one in the brotherhood of stone,
Bound together in hardness and in weakness,
The ancient dead have escaped the circle and risen again
Smiling in a strange silence.

XXII

Because so many things have passed before our eyes
That even our eyes saw nothing but beyond,
And behind us memory like the white screen one night in a walled place
On which we saw strange images, more strange than you,
Passing and fading in the unstirring foliage of a pepper tree;

Because we have known so well this fate of ours,
Wandering among broken stones, three or six thousand years,
Digging in ruined buildings which could have been, perhaps, our homes,
Trying to remember dates and deeds of heroes;
Shall we be able?

Because we have been bound, because we have been scattered,
And have struggled with difficulties described as non-existent,
Lost, then finding again a road full of blind battalions,
Sinking in marshes and in the lake of Marathon,
Shall we be able to die in a normal way?

XXIII

Just a little more
And we shall see the almond trees in blossom
The marbles shining in the sun
The sea, the curling waves.

Just a little more
Let us rise just a little higher.

XXIV

Here end the works of the sea, the works of love.
Those who one day shall live here where we end,
If ever the dark blood should rise to overflow their memory,
Let them not forget us, the strengthless souls among the asphodels.
Let them turn towards Erebus the heads of the victims.
We who had nothing shall teach them peace.

II

GYMNOPAEDIA

'Santorin is geologically composed of
pumice-stone and china-clay; in her bay
islands have appeared and disappeared.
This island was once the birthplace of a
very ancient religion. The lyrical dance
of a strict and heavy rythm performed
here was called: *Gymnopaedia.*'

Guide to Greece

I. Santorin

Stoop down, if you can, to the dark sea, forgetting
The sound of a flute played to naked feet
That tread your sleep in the other life, the submerged one.

Write, if you can, upon your last shell
The day, the name, the place
The throw it into the sea that it may sink.

We found ourselves naked on the pumice stone
Watching the islands rising out of the sea,
Watching the red islands sinking
In their sleep, in our sleep.
Here we stood naked holding
The scales weighted in favour of injustice.

Instep of power, unshadowed will, considered love,
Plans ripening beneath the sun of midday
And course of fate at the clap of a young hand
Upon the shoulder;
In the place that crumbled, that makes no resistance,
In the place that was once our own,
Ashes and rust the islands sink.

Altars in ruins
And friends forgotten
Leaves of palm in mud.

Let your hands, if you can, go travelling
Here on the turn of time with that far ship
Which has touched the horizon.
When the dice struck upon the slab
When the spear struck the breastplate
When the eye recognised the stranger
And love drained out
In pierced souls;
When you look round and you find
All about you swathes of feet
All about you dead hands
All about you darkened eyes;
When there is no longer any choice
Of the death you wanted as your own,
Listening to a great cry,
Even to a wolf that yells——
Your due;
Let your hands, if you can, go travelling;
Tear yourself loose from the unfaithful time
And sink.

Needs must he sink who carries the great stones.

II. Mycenae

Give me your hands, give me your hands, give me your hands
I saw in the night
The mountain's pointed peak
I saw the plain afar flooded in moonlight
And no moon to be seen;
I saw, turning my head,
Black stones huddled around
And all my life stretched out like a string,
The beginning and the ending,
The final moment
My hands.

Needs must he sink who carries the great stones;
These stones I have carried as long as I was able,
These stones I have loved as long as I was able,
These stones my fate.
Wounded by my own soil
Tortured by my own garment
Condemned by my own gods,
These stones.

I know they do not know; yet I
Who have so often followed
The path that leads from murderer to victim
From victim to the punishment
And from the punishment up to another murder;

Groping my way
Over the purple welling inexhaustible
That night of the return
When the whistling began
Of Furies in the scanty grass——
I have seen snakes crossed with vipers
Knotted about the accursed generation
Our fate.

Voices out of stone, out of sleep,
Voices more deep here where the world grows dark,
Memory of toil that is rooted in the rhythm
Beaten upon the earth by feet forgotten.
Bodies sunk, all naked, in the foundations
Of the other time. Eyes
Staring and staring towards a sign
That you, however you wish it, cannot distinguish.
The soul
That fights to become your soul.

Even the silence is no longer yours
Here where the mill stones have stopped still.

III

FROM AN EXERCISE-BOOK

Haiku

I

Pour into the lake
Only a wine drop
And the sun's gone.

II

In the Museum garden

Chairs empty
Statues returned
To the other museum.

III

Is this the voice
Of our dead friends
Or of the gramophone?

IV

What's wrong with the rudder?
The boat goes in circles
And not one gull.

V

This column has
A hole. Can you see
The Queen of the Dead?

VI

How hard to collect
The thousand fragments
Of each and every man!

VII

Ailing Fury

Now she's eyeless.
The snakes she held once
Eat up her hands.

VIII

As you are writing
The ink grows less
The sea increases.

Stratis the Sailor Describes a Man

1.

But what's the matter with this man?
All through the afternoon (yesterday, the day before yesterday and today)
      he has been sitting with his eyes fixed upon a flame.
In the evening he bumped into me on his way downstairs.
He said:
'The body dies, water turns cloudy, the soul
Hesitates
And the wind forgets, the wind is always forgetting,
But the flame does not change.'
He also said to me:
'You know I love a woman who has gone away, possibly to the world below.
      But that is not why I look so deserted.
I am trying to hold myself in from a flame,
Because it does not change.'
Then he told me the story of his life.

2. Child

When I started to grow up, I was tortured by the trees.
Why do you smile? Were you thinking of spring, which is cruel to children?
I was very fond of the green leaves;
I think I learnt a few things at school because the blotting paper on my desk
      was green too.
It was the roots of the trees that tortured me, when in the winter warmth
      they came to twine about my body.

These were the only dreams I had in childhood.
In this way I became acquainted with my body.

3. *Adolescent*

In the summer of my sixteenth year a strange voice sang in my ears.
I was standing, I remember, by the sea's edge, among the red nets and the
  shell of an abandoned boat like a skeleton.
I tried to get nearer to that voice by putting my ear down on the sand.
The voice vanished
But a shooting star
As though I had never seen a shooting star before,
And on my lips the salt taste of the waves.
That night the roots of the trees no longer came.
Next day a voyage unfolded in my mind, then shut again like a picture book.
I thought of going down every evening to the shore
To learn first about the shore and then to take to the sea.
On the third day I fell in love with a girl on a hill;
She had a little white house like a mountain chapel;
An old mother by the window, spectacles bent over the knitting
Never a word,
A pot of basil, a pot of carnations.
She was called, I think, Vasso, Frosso or Bilio;
So I forgot the sea.
One Monday in October
I found a broken jar in front of the little white house.
Vasso (let us say for short) appeared in a black dress,
Her hair disordered, her eyes red.

To my question she replied:

'She is dead; the doctor says she died because we didn't slaughter the
    black cock on the foundations. . . . How could we get hold of a black
    cock here? . . . There is nothing except white flocks . . . and the
    poultry in the market are sold already plucked.'
This was not how I had imagined grief and death.
I left and went back to the sea.
That night on the deck of the *St. Nicholas*
I dreamed of a very old olive tree in tears.

4. Young man
I sailed for one year with Captain Odysseus.
I felt fine.
In fair weather I would settle down in the prow next to the siren figure-head;
I sang of her red lips while I stared at the flying-fish.
When it was rough I huddled up in a corner of the hold with the ship's dog
    to keep me warm.
At the end of the year one morning I saw minarets.
The ship's mate said:
'That is Saint Sophia. Tonight I'll take you to find some girls.'
So I came to know those women who wear only stockings,
The ones we choose, yes, those ones.
It was a funny sort of place,
A garden with two walnut-trees, a vine-trellis, a well
And a wall all round with broken glass on the top.
A ditch was singing 'On the stream of my life.'
Then I saw for the first time a heart

[45]

Pierced by the famous arrow.
It was drawn on the wall with a piece of charcoal.
I saw the leaves of the vine
Fallen to the earth, all yellow,
Plastered to the paving stones in the wretched mud,
And I made a step to go back again to the ship.
Then the mate took me by the collar and threw me into the well;
Warm water, and so much life all round the skin.
Afterwards the girl told me, while she was playing idly with her right breast,
'I come from Rhodes. They betrothed me at thirteen for a hundred paras.'
And the ditch was singing 'On the stream of my life. . . .'
I remembered the broken jar in the cool afternoon and I thought
'She too will die. How will she die?'
But all I said to her was
'Look out, or you will spoil it. It's your livelihood.'
That night on the ship I did not dare go near the siren;
       I was ashamed of her.

5. *Man*

Since then I have seen many new landscapes: green plains joining earth with heaven and man with seed in an unbearable dampness; planes and firs; lakes with wrinkled visions and swans immortal for having lost their voice—pieces of scenery unfolded before my eyes by that headstrong companion of mine, that strolling player, while he blew great blasts on the long horn which had ruined his lips and which, with its shrill stridency, brought crashing down, like the trumpet at Jericho, whatever I might just have had the time to build. I also saw an old painting in a low-ceilinged

[46]

room; there was a crowd of people admiring it. It represented the raising of Lazarus from the dead. I don't remember the Christ or the Lazarus. Only, in a corner, the disgust painted on a face that was looking at the miracle as though smelling it. He was trying to protect his mouth with a huge piece of cloth that was hanging from his head-dress. This gentleman of the 'Renaissance' taught me not to expect much from the Second Coming.

> They told us, you will conquer when you submit.
> We submitted and found dust and ashes.
> They told us, you will conquer when you love.
> We loved and found dust and ashes.
> They told us, you will conquer when you give up your life.
> We gave up our life and found dust and ashes.

We found dust and ashes. It remains to rediscover our life now that we have nothing left any more. I imagine that he who rediscovers life out of so many papers, so many emotions, so many quarrels and so many teachings, will be someone quite like us; only he will be a little tougher so far as memory is concerned. We (we can't help it) still remember what we have given. He will only remember what he gained from each of his offerings. What can a flame remember? If it remembers a little less than it needs, it just goes out. If it remembers a little more than it needs, it just goes out; if only it could teach us, during the time that it burns, to remember aright. I have reached the end. If only it were possible at least that someone else might start from the point where I ended. There are moments when I have the impression that I have arrived at the goal, that everything is in its proper place, ready to sing together in accord. The machine just on the point of starting. In fact

I can imagine it actually in motion, a living thing, like something astonishingly new. But there is still something else; an infinitesimal impediment, a grain of sand, which grows smaller and smaller, but never so small as to disappear entirely. I do not know what I should say or what I should do. This impediment sometimes seems to me like a tear drop which has become lodged in some articulation of the orchestra and which, until it can be dissolved, will keep every instrument dumb. And I have the unbearable feeling that all the rest of my life will not be enough to dissolve this drop within my soul. And I am haunted by the thought that, if they were to burn me alive, the last part of me to surrender would be this insistent moment.

Who is there to help us? Once, when I was still working as a seaman (it was in July at noon) I found myself alone on an island, an invalid in the sun. From the sea a gentle breeze was blowing, bringing thoughts of tenderness, and just then a couple came and sat down not far away,—a young woman whose transparent dress revealed the lines of her body, slim and full of spirit, like a gazelle's, and a man, quite silent, who, from a distance of two yards, was looking into her eyes. They were speaking in a language I did not know. She was calling him 'Jim.' However their words had no weight; and their looks, intertwined and still, left their eyes blind. I keep thinking of them because they are the only human beings I have ever seen who did not have that rapacious or hunted look which I have observed in everyone else. That look which places them either in the pack of wolves or in the flock of sheep. I met this couple again the same day in one of those little chapels which one finds on the islands, stumbling upon them and losing them again as soon as one gets out. They were still keeping at the same distance from each other, and then they drew close and kissed. The woman became a cloudy shape, and being so small, vanished. I wondered whether they knew that they had escaped from the nets of the world. . . .

It is time for me to go. I know a pine tree that leans over near a sea. At mid-day it bestows upon the tired body a shade measured like our life, and in the evening the wind blowing through its needles begins a curious song as though of souls that have made an end of death, just at the moment when they begin to become skin and lips again. Once I stayed awake all night under this tree. At dawn I was new, as though I had been freshly quarried.

If only one could live like this, it doesn't matter.

London, June 1932

Two of His Epigrams

I

This gentleman
Every morning has his bath
In the waters of the Dead Sea,
Then puts on a bitter smile
For the business and for the customers.

II

We forgot our heroic contest with the Eumenides;
Sleep overcame us, they took us for dead
And they left, shouting:
'I—ow! I—ow! . . . Pew—pax! . . .'
Cursing the gods who were protecting us.

In the Manner of G. S.

Wherever I travel Greece keeps wounding me.

On Pelion beneath the chestnuts the Centaur's shirt
Slid through the leaves to wind about my body
As I climbed up the slope and the sea came after me,
Rising, like mercury in a thermometer,
Until we found the mountain waters.
At Santorin, touching the sinking islands,
Hearing a pipe play somewhere on the pumice stone,
My hand was nailed to the gunwale
By an arrow suddenly shot
From the extreme end of departed youth.
At Mycenae I lifted up the great boulders
And the treasures of the sons of Atreus,
And slept beside them in the hotel 'Belle Helène.'
They only left in the morning when Cassandra crowed
With a cock hanging down from her black throat.
At Spetsai at Poros and at Mykonos
I was nauseated by the barcaroles.

What are they after, all those people who suppose
Themselves to be in Athens or Piraeus?
One comes from Salamis and asks another
'You have come, I imagine, from Concord Square?' 'Oh no'
Replies the other, pleased, 'From the Constitution.
'I met old John there. He stood me an ice.'

Meanwhile Greece travels onwards
And we know nothing, we do not know that all of us
Are sailors with no ships, we do not know
The bitterness of harbours when every ship has gone;
We mock at those who actually experience this.
Strange, people who say they are in Attica and are nowhere;
They buy the sugared almonds to get married;
In their hands they hold scalp lotions; they are photographed:
There was a man I saw this morning, sitting
Against a background of pigeons and of flowers,
Accepting the hand of the old photographer
That smoothed out from his face the wrinkles
Left upon it by all the fowls of the air.

Meanwhile Greece travels onwards, always travels,
And if we see 'the Aegean flower with corpses'
They are those who tried to swim after the big ship and catch it,
Those who got tired of waiting for ships that would not sail,
The *Elsie*, the *Samothrace*, the *Ambraciot*.
Ships whistle now as night falls on Piraeus;
They whistle and whistle again, but no capstan moves,
No wet chain has shone in the last ray of twilight,
The captain stands in white and gold like a stone.

Wherever I travel, Greece keeps wounding me,
Curtains of mountains, archipelagos, naked granite.
They call the ship which travels,—AGONY 937.

A Word for Summer

We are back again in autumn. Summer,
Like a copybook which has wearied us, remains
Full of words crossed out, pen strokes scribbled in the margin
And question marks. We are back again
In the season of the eyes which gaze
Into the mirror below the electric light,
Tightened lips and the people strangers
In rooms, in streets, under the pepper trees,
While the headlights of motorcars destroy
The livid masks of faces in their thousands.
We are back again; when we start we always get back
To solitude, a handful of earth in empty palms.

And yet I once loved Syngros Avenue
The double lullaby of the wide road
That would leave us miraculously by the sea
The eternal sea to cleanse us of our sins;
I have loved men unknown
Encountered suddenly at the end of the day
Speaking to themselves like captains of a sunken armada
An indication that the world is wide.
And yet I have loved the roads here and these columns,
Though I was born on the other shore
Near reeds and rushes, islands
With fresh water welling from the sand for the rower
To quench his thirst; though I was born near

The sea which I wind and unwind on my fingers
When I am tired,—I know no longer where I was born.

There still remains summer the yellow essence
And your hands touching the sea-bells in the water,
Your eyes unveiled suddenly, the first eyes
Of the world, and the marine caves,
Bare feet on the red earth.
There still remains summer the fair haired marble youth,
A little salt that has dried in the hollow of a rock,
A few pine needles after the rain
Raggedly strewn and red like tattered nets.

I don't understand these faces I don't understand them.
Sometimes they imitate death and then again
They gleam with the humble life of the glow-worm,
With a restricted effort, hopeless,
Compressed between two wrinkles
Between two café tables covered with stains,
They kill one another they grow smaller,
They stick to the panes of glass like postage stamps
The faces of the other tribe.

We walked together we shared bread and sleep
We felt the same bitterness of parting
We built our houses with the stones that we had by us
We took to the ships, we went abroad; we returned;
We found our wives waiting for us;

They recognised us with difficulty, nobody recognises us.
And our comrades wore the statues they wore the bare
And empty chairs of autumn, and our comrades
Did away with their faces; I don't understand them.
There still remains summer, the yellow desert;
Waves of sand receding to the last circle,
A drum beat without pity, without end,
Blood shot eyes sinking into the sun,
Hands in the manner of birds streaking the sky,
Saluting ranks of dead who stand to attention,
Hands lost to a point beyond my control though it dominates me,
Your hands touching the free wave.

Epitaph

The coals in the fog
Were roses rooted in your heart,
And every morning the ashes covered your face.

Plucking shadows from cypresses
You went away that summer.

Cease Now

Cease now to look for the sea and the waves' fleece driving the ships on.
Under the sky it is we who are fish and the trees are the seaweeds.

IV

FROM LOGBOOK I

'Hove-to. Awaiting instructions.'
Log Books, passim.

Mathios Paschalis among the Roses

I have been smoking since morning without a break;
If I stop the roses will take me in their embrace,
With thorns and with fallen petals they will choke me.
They grow crookedly all of them with the same pink colour;
They are staring; they are waiting for someone; no one comes.
Behind the smoke of my pipe I watch them
On a bored stalk, without scent;
In the other life a woman used to say to me: you can touch this hand
And it is yours this rose, it is yours you can take it
Now or later, whenever you like.

Still smoking, I go down the garden steps
And the roses come down with me. They are excited;
They have something in their manner of that voice
At the root of the cry, at the point where man begins
To shout out 'Mother!' or 'Help!',
Or the small white cries of love.

It is a small garden full of roses,
A few square yards that come along down with me
As I descend the steps, without the sky.
And her aunt was saying to her 'Antigone,
Today you forgot to do your exercises.
At your age I never wore a corset. Not in my time'.
Her aunt was a poor old body,—veins in relief,
Many wrinkles round her ears, a nose about to die;

Yet her words always full of wisdom.
One day I saw her touching Antigone's breast,
Like a child stealing an apple.

Will I perhaps meet the old woman as I keep descending?
When I left she said to me 'Who knows when we shall meet again?'
Then I read of her death in some old newspapers
And of Antigone's wedding and the wedding of Antigone's daughter
Without an end of the steps or of my tobacco
Which imparts to me the taste of a haunted ship
With a mermaid crucified, when still beautiful, to the wheel.

Our own Sun

This sun was mine and it was yours: we shared it.
Who is in pain behind the golden curtain? Who is dying?
A woman cried out, beating her dry breasts: 'Cowards,
They have taken my children and torn them into pieces.
You killed them, looking in the evening at the fire-flies
With that strange look, lost in blind contemplation.'
Green light of a tree on a hand where blood was drying;
A sleeping warrior grasping a lance that flared against his side.

This sun was ours. We saw nothing behind the gold embroidery.
Later the messengers came, breathless and dirty,
Stammering out unintelligible words;
Twenty days and nights on barren ground and only thorns
Twenty days and nights huddled to the bleeding bellies of horses
And not one moment to halt and drink the rain water.
You told them to rest first and talk afterwards;
The light had blinded you.
They died saying 'We have no time'; some rays of sun they touched.
You had forgotten that no one ever rests.

A woman howled 'Cowards!' like a dog in the night.
She must have once been beautiful as you,
With moist lips, living veins beneath the skin,
With love—

This sun was ours; you kept it all; you did not want to follow me.
And then I learned these things behind the golden curtain.
We have no time. The messengers were right.

[61]

The Return of the Exile

'Old friend, what are you looking for?
After those many years abroad you come
With images you tended
Under foreign skies
Far away from your own land.'

'I look for my old garden;
The trees come only to my waist,
The hills seem low as terraces;
Yet when I was a child
I played there on the grass
Underneath great shadows
And used to run across the slopes
For hours and hours, breathless.'

'My old friend, rest a little.
You will soon get used to it.
Together we will climb
The hill paths that you know;
Together we will sit and rest
Underneath the plane trees' dome;
Little by little they'll come back to you,
Your garden and your slopes.'

'I look for my old house,
The house with the tall windows

Darkened by the ivy,
And for that ancient column
The landmark of the sailor.
How can I get into this hutch?
The roof's below my shoulders
And however far I look
I see men on their knees;
You'd say that they were praying.'

'My old friend, can't you hear me?
You will soon get used to it.
Here is your house in front of you,
And at this door will soon come knocking
Your friends and your relations
To give you a fine welcome.'

'Why is your voice so far away?
Raise your head a little higher
That I may grasp the words you say,
For as you speak you seem to grow
Shorter still and shorter
As though you were sinking down into the ground.'

'My old friend, just think a little.
You will soon get used to it;
Your homesickness has built for you
A non-existent land with laws
Outside the earth and man.'

[63]

'Now I hear nothing,—not a sound.
My last friend too has sunk and gone.
How strange it is, this levelling
All around from time to time:
They pass and mow here
Thousands of scythe-bearing chariots.'

Interval of Joy

All through that morning we were full of joy,
My God, how full of joy!
Stones leaves flowers shone first;
And then the sun,
An enormous sun, all thorns, but so high up in the sky.
A nymph was gathering our cares; she hung them on the trees;
It was a wood of Judas trees.
Young Loves and satyrs sported there and sang;
And through black laurel leaves one caught the rosy gleam
Of little children's limbs.
All through the morning we were full of joy;
The abyss was a closed well and above it
Beat the tender foot of an infant faun.
Do you remember his laugh? How full of joy!
Then the clouds, rain and the damp earth.
You stopped laughing when you lay down in the hut;
With your great eyes wide open you looked upon
The archangel exercising with a fiery sword——

'I can't explain it', you said, 'I can't explain.
I find people impossible to understand.
Play with colours as they will, they all are black.'

The Last Day

The day was cloudy. No one could make up his mind.
A light wind blew. 'North east' someone said 'a touch of south'.
A few slim cypresses nailed on the slope; the sea,
A little further, was grey with shining pools.
The troops were presenting arms as it started to drizzle.
'The wind is not north-east; it is south east——';
That was the only definite thing that was heard.
And yet we knew that tomorrow there would be left to us
Nothing at all, not even the woman beside us drinking sleep,
Not even the memory that once we were men,
By tomorrow's dawn nothing at all any more.

'This wind reminds me of the spring' she said,
My friend walking beside me, looking into the distance, 'the spring
That suddenly came in winter by the shut-in sea.
So unexpected. So many years have passed
Since then. How shall we die?'

A funeral march moved by in the thin rain.
How does a man die? Strange that no one thought of this.
Or if one did, it was as a recollection from ancient chronicles,
The Crusades, perhaps, or the sea-battle fought at Salamis.
And yet death is a thing that happens. How does a man die?
And yet one wins one's death, which is one's own and nobody else's,
And this kind of game is life.
The light was sinking from the clouded day. No one made up his mind.

Tomorrow there would be left to us nothing at all,——
Everything surrendered,—not even our hands,
And our women working for strangers at the water springs,
Our children at the quarries.
My friend, walking beside me, was singing a snatch of song
'In spring, in summer, slaves. . . .'
One could remember old teachers who left us orphaned.
A couple passed us, talking,
'I am sick and tired of the dusk. Let's go.
Let us go home now and turn on the light.'

February 1939

Spring A.D.

Again with the spring
She wore light colours
With a weightless walking
Again with the spring
Again with the summer
She was smiling.

Breast among fresh shoots
To the veins all naked
Beyond night's dryness
Beyond the white old men
Debating in whispers
Which would be better
To surrender the keys
Or pull hard on the rope
Hang themselves from the noose
And to leave empty bodies
Where the souls could not hold out
Where the mind could not catch up
And the knees were failing.

When the new shoots were bursting
The old men failed.
They surrendered everything
Grand-children great-grandchildren
The tilth of the pastures

[68]

The green of the mountains
Both love and livelihood
Both mercy and roof
Both rivers and sea;
They departed like statues
Leaving silence behind them
That was cut by no sword stroke
Broken by no galloping
Or voices of young men;
And there came the great solitude
The great deprivation
In this spring's company
It settled, it spread
Like the morning's hoar-frost
Taking hold on high branches
Sliding down among tree trunks
And enfolded our soul.

But she smiled
As she wore light colours
Like an almond flowering
Among yellow flames
In her weightless walking
Opening windows
In rejoicing sky
Out of the company
Of us the ill-fated ones.
And I saw her breast naked

The waist and the knee
As rises from torture
On the way to the heavens
Untouched, clean, the martyr,
Away from the people's
Indecipherable whispering
In the enormous arena,
Away from the black scowl
The sweat-streaming shoulders
Of the executioner
Striking indignantly
Since his strokes achieve nothing.
Like the lake's surface
Became the solitude
Like the lake's surface
Became the deprivation
Untouched and traceless.

The King of Asine

'Ασίνην τε . . . The Iliad

All that morning we looked at the citadel from every angle.
We began from the side in the shadow, where the sea,
Green, without brilliance,—breast of a slain peacock,
Received us like time that has no break in it.
From high above the veins in the rock descended,
Twisted vines leafless, many branched, regaining life
At the touch of water, while the eye, following them,
Strove to escape the weary rocking motion
And gradually lost strength.

On the sunny side a long and open beach
And the light polishing jewels on the massy walls.
No living creature; the wild pigeons had gone,
And the King of Asine, our quest for two years now,
Unknown, forgotten by everyone, even by Homer——
Just one word in the Iliad and that word doubtful
Thrown down here like the gold sepulchral mask.
You tapped it. Do you remember how it rang?
Hollow in the light, like a dry jar in dug earth.
And our oars in the sea made the same sound.
The King of Asine an emptiness beneath the mask,
Everywhere with us, everywhere with us, beneath a name:

"*'Ασίνην τε . . . 'Ασίνην τε . . .*"
And his children statues,

And his desires the beat of birds' wings and the wind
Blowing through the spaces of his thoughts, and his ships
Moored in a vanished harbour;
Under the mask an emptiness.

Behind the great eyes, the curved lips, the curling locks
Embossed on the gold covering of our lives,
A moving darkness, swimming like the fish
In the dawn calm of the sea, and you are watching it,
An emptiness everywhere with us.
And the bird that flew away the other winter
With a broken wing,
The sanctuary of life,
And the young woman who went off to play
With the dogs' teeth of summer,
And the soul which, twittering, sought the underworld,
And the country like a great plane-leaf dragged down
By the torrent of the sun,
With the ancient monuments and the present sorrow.

And the poet lingers, looks at the stones and asks himself:
Do they still exist, then,
Among these broken lines, edges, points, hollows, curves,
Do they still exist
Here at the meeting place of rain, wind, ruin,
Do they exist, the movement of the face,
The form and fashion of the tenderness
Of those who so strangely have dwindled in our life,

Of those who remained shadows of waves and thoughts
With the limitless expanse of the open sea?
Or no, perhaps what remains is only the weight,
The craving for the weight of a living creature
Here where we now remain unsubstantial, leaning over,
Like twigs of the dreadful willow heaped together in the continuity of
     hopelessness
While slowly the yellow stream bears down mud with uprooted reeds,
Image of a face that has turned to stone with the decision of an everlasting
     bitterness.
The poet an emptiness.

Shield-bearing the sun was climbing like a warrior
And from the depths of the cave a frightened bat
Struck upon the light as an arrow strikes a buckler—
"᾿Ασίνην τε . . . ᾿Ασίνην τε . . ."
                                 Could this have been
The King of Asine for whom with such great care
We searched as we went about this acropolis,
Feeling sometimes with our fingers his very touch upon the stones?

V

FROM LOGBOOK II

─────

FOR MARO

Days of June 1941

The new moon rose over Alexandria
Holding the old one in her arms
And we on our way towards the Gate of the Sun
In the night of the heart,—three friends.

We sought in our youth the metamorphosis
With desires that flashed like big fishes
In seas that suddenly shrunk:
We used to believe in the omnipotence of the body.
And now the new moon has risen in embrace
With the old moon; and the beautiful island lies
Wounded and bleeding, the calm island, the strong, the innocent.
And the bodies like broken branches
And like roots torn from the ground.
                                        Our thirst

The statue of a horseman
At the dark Gate of the Sun
Does not know what to ask for; stands upon guard
In exile hereabouts
Near to the burial place of Alexander.

Postscript

September 11, 1941

But they have eyes all white, without eyelashes,
And their arms are thin as reeds.

Lord, not with these. I have known
The voice of children at dawn
Running on green hillsides
Happily coloured, like the bees
And like the butterflies.
Lord, not with these, their voice
Cannot even leave their mouths.
It stays there glued on yellow teeth.

Yours the sea and the wind
With a star hung in the firmament;
Lord, they do not know that we are
What we are able to be,
Healing our wounds with the herbs
That we find on the green hillsides,
These ones, near us, not others;
That we breathe as we are able to breathe
With a small supplication each morning
That reaches the shore, travelling
In memory's chasms.
Lord, not with these; Let thy will be done in another way.

[78]

Stratis the Sailor among the Agapanthi

There are no asphodels, violets, or hyacinths;
How is one to speak with the dead?
The dead only know the language of flowers,
For that reason they keep silent;
They go their ways in silence, they endure in silence,
In the city of dreams,—in the city of dreams.

If I start singing, I shall shout
And if I shout——
The agapanthi command silence,
Raising the tiny hand
Of some blue-skinned Arabian child
Or footprints of a goose upon the air.

Heavy the task and hard,—the living are not enough,
First because they do not speak, and then
Because I have to ask the dead
In order to be able to go further.
Otherwise it is impossible. If I fall asleep
My comrades go and cut the silver cords
And the bag that held the winds is emptied.
I fill it; it empties. I fill it and it empties.
I wake up
Like the goldfish swimming
Into gaps of lightning,
And the wind and the flood and the human bodies

And the agapanthi stuck like the arrows of fate
In the insatiable earth
Shaken by beckoning spasms,
One would say they were loaded on a very old cart
Jolting in pot-holes down old cobbled roads,
The agapanthi, asphodels of the negroes;
How am I to become acquainted with this religion?

The first thing God made is love
Then comes the blood
And the thirst for blood
Goaded by the body's seed as if by salt.
The first thing God made is the long journey;
That house is waiting
With its blue smoke,
With the dog grown old
Waiting, that he may die, for the homecoming.
But the dead must give me guidance;
It is the agapanthi which hold them speechless
Like the depths of the sea or the water in a glass.
And the comrades stay on in the palaces of Circe;
My dear Elpenor! My poor, idiotic Elpenor!
Or do you not see them?
——'Help us!'——
At Psara on the blackened slope.

An Old Man on the River Bank

And yet we ought to consider how we go forward;
Feeling is not enough, nor thought, nor movement,
Nor risking life and limb in the old embrasure
When boiling oil and molten lead come furrowing down the walls.
And yet we ought to consider where we are going;
Not as our pain would have it and our starving children
And the gulf of calling from friends across the sea,
Nor as it may be whispered by the bluish night-light in a camp surgery,
The clinical glow on the pillow of the young man operated upon at noon;
But in some other way: perhaps what I want to say is—like
The long river descending from the great lakes shut in the depths of
     Africa
And which was once a god, and then became a road, a giver, a judge, and
     a delta,
Which is never the same (just as the old scholars taught)
And yet keeps always the same body and structure,
Is the same as Symbol,
The same in orientation.

All I want is to speak simply; for this grace I pray.
For we have loaded even the song with so many kinds of music
That gradually it sinks.
And our art we so decorated that beneath the gilt
Its face is eaten away.
And it is now time for us to say the few words we have to say
Because tomorrow our soul sets sail.

If pain is man's lot, we were not born men
Only that we should suffer;
That is why these days I think so much of the great river,
Of that meaning pushing forward through reeds and rushes,
Among the beasts that feed and drink, among the men who sow and reap
And also among mighty tombs and little dwelling-places of the dead.
That stream which goes its way and is not so different from the blood of
    men
Or from the eyes of men when, with no fear in their hearts, they look
    directly forwards
With none of the daily trembling at trifles or even at important things,
Looking straight ahead, like the wayfarer accustomed to plot his journey
    by the stars,
Not like us, the other day, looking into the enclosed garden of the sleeping
    Arab house,
Behind the trellises the fresh little garden changing shape, growing larger
    and smaller,
And we too changing as we looked, the shape of our desire and of our
    hearts,
At the height of noon, we the patient dough kneaded by a world which
    drives us out,
Caught in the gaudy nets of a life which was right and turned to dust and
    sank into the sand,
Leaving behind it just that indefinite rocking of a tall palm, which made
    us giddy.

Stratis the Sailor by the Dead Sea

Sometimes you see, in chapels built upon the legendary spots, the relevant passage from the Gospel, in English, and underneath the words: THIS IS THE PLACE GENTLEMEN.

Letter of S.S. from Jerusalem, 22nd July, 1942

Jerusalem, ungoverned city,
Jerusalem, city of the refugee.

Sometimes you see at noon
On asphalt of the road go slipping
A flock of black leaves scattered——
They go by, the birds of passage under the sun,
But you do not raise your head.

Jerusalem, ungoverned city.

Unknown tongues from Babel
With no relation to the grammar
To the Life of the Saints or to the Psalter
Which once they taught you to spell out in autumn
When they tied up the fishing boats to the quays;
Unknown tongues stuck fast
Like old cigarette-butts upon broken lips.

Jerusalem, city of the refugee.

But their eyes all speak the same word,
Not, God forgive us, the Word that became Man,

Not travelling to see new places, but
The dark train of escape, where babies
Feed upon the filth and the sins of parents
And the middle-aged feel growing wider
The gap between the body
That drags behind them like a wounded camel
And the soul with its courage inexhaustible, as they say.
There are also the ships that carry them
Upright, like embalmed bishops, in the holds,
So that one evening they may come to anchorage
On the sea bottom, among the weeds there, gently.

Jerusalem, ungoverned city.

Down to the river Jordan
Came three holy monks,
And tied up to the bank there
A small red sailing ship.
Three from the Holy Mountain,
Sailing for three months,
Came to the bank of Jordan
And tied on to a branch
Their votive offering,
A gift of the refugee.
Three months without food,
Three months without drink,
Three months without sleep,
And they came from the Holy Mountain,

They came from Thessaloniki,
The three slave monks.

All of us are like the Dead Sea
Many fathoms below the level of the Aegean.
Come with me. I shall show you what the place is like.

Down in the Dead Sea
There are no fishes
There are no sea weeds
No sea urchins
There is no life.
There are no creatures
Feeding stomachs
Able to hunger
Feeding nerves
Able to feel pain.

THIS IS THE PLACE GENTLEMEN . . .
Down in the Dead Sea
Cruel contempt
Is not the business
Of any person,
Nobody cares.
The heart and the mind
Grow stiff in the salt,
The bitter salt;
They take their places
Among the minerals.

[85]

THIS IS THE PLACE GENTLEMEN . . .

Down in the Dead Sea
Friend and enemy,
Children, wife,
Uncles and cousins,
Go and find them.
They stay in Gomorrah
Down at the bottom
Perfectly happy
In not expecting
Any signal.

GENTLEMEN,

We will now continue our tour
Many fathoms below the level of the Aegean.

Last Stop

Not many moon-lit nights have given me pleasure.
The alphabet of stars which you spell out
So far as fatigue at the end of the day allows,
Disentangling different meanings and different hopes,
This you can read more clearly.
Now that I sit down idly and reckon it up,
Not many moons have remained in my memory——
Islands, colour of the Virgin in her affliction, late in waning,
Or moonlight in cities of the north, shedding sometimes
Over the throng of streets, over rivers and the limbs of men
A heavy weight of torpor.
Yet yesterday evening here on this last stage of our journey
Where we wait for the hour of our return to dawn
Like a debt long owed, money that has stayed for ages
In the chest of a miser, and finally
There has come the moment of payment, and you hear
The chink of coins falling upon the table;
In this Etruscan village behind the sea of Salerno,
Behind the harbours of our return, at the edge
Of an autumn shower, the moon
Broke through the clouds and on the opposite shore
The houses became enamelled.
Amica silentia lunae.

This also is a chain of thought, a way
To begin to speak of things you find hard to confess,

In helpless silent moments, to a friend
Who got away and brings
News from home and news from comrades,
And you must hurry to open your heart in time,
Before the foreign country forestalls you and alters him.
We come from Arab Lands; Egypt, Palestine, Syria;
The tiny Kingdom
Of Commagene which has flickered out like a night-light
Often comes back to mind,
And mighty cities living for thousands of years,
Afterwards ground for the pasturing of oxen,
Flat territories for sugar cane or maize.
We come from desert sands and from the sea of Proteus,
Souls shrivelled up by public sins,
Each one his rank and position, like a bird in its cage.
The rainy autumn in this hollow place
Rots and turns septic each man's private wound;
Or you may choose a different word,—fate, nemesis,
Or just bad habits, fraud and treachery
Or even the selfishness that makes profit from others' blood.
Man is easily worn out in warfare;
Man is soft, a bundle of grass;
Lips and fingers hungering for a white breast,
Eyes half-shut to the glare of the day,
And feet that will run, however tired they may be,
Towards the least whisper of profit.
Man is soft and thirsty like grass,
Insatiable as grass with nerves spreading like roots.

When harvest comes
He would rather hear the scythes whistle in the next man's field.
When harvest comes
Some cry out to exorcise the fiend,
Some get entangled in their property
And some make speeches.
But what can you do with all your exorcisms,
With all your property and all your speeches
When those who are alive are far away?
May it not be that man is something different?
Is it not just this that confers life?
A time for sowing and a time for the harvest.

Again and again the same things, you will tell me, friend;
Yet the thought of the exile, the thought of the prisoner, the thought
Of man, when man has become a commodity,——
Try to alter it, you cannot.
Perhaps, even, he would like to remain King of the Cannibals,
Using up powers which no one wants to buy,
To walk among broad fields of agapanthi,
To hear the drums beneath the bamboo tree
As the courtiers, wierdly masked, step in the dance.
Nevertheless the country under the axe, chopped,
        burned like pine, and you see it,
Whether in the dark compartment, without water, the windows
        broken, night after night,
Or in the red-hot ship which, according to statistics, will sink——
These things are fixed in the mind; they do not change;

These things have planted images, like those trees
Which drop their shoots down in the virgin forest,
And these take root in the earth then rise and then
Throw down more shoots and again rise, bestriding
League after league.
Our mind is a virgin forest of murdered friends.
And if I speak to you in fables and parables
It is for your smoother hearing, and horror
Cannot be spoken because it is alive,
Because it is silent and is going forward;
It drips into the day and it drips into sleep
Sorrow-recalling pain.

To speak of heroes, to speak of heroes. Michael
Who with open wounds fled from the hospital,——
Perhaps he spoke of heroes when, that night,
As he dragged his feet along through blacked-out streets,
He howled groping over our pain, 'Into the darkness
We go, into the darkness we go forward. . . .'
Heroes go forward into darkness.

Not many moon-lit nights have given me pleasure.

Cava dei Tirreni, October, 1944

VI

THE 'THRUSH'

———

'Shortlived offspring of a cruel daemon
and a hard fate, why do you force me to
speak of things which it would be
better for you not to know.'

Silenus to Midas

I

The House near the Sea

The houses that I had they took from me. It happened
The times were out of joint. Wars, waste and exiles.
Sometimes the hunter gets the birds of passage
Sometimes he does not get them. There was in my time
Good hunting. Burst of fire took a heavy toll.
The others turn round and round or go mad in the shelters.

Do not speak to me of the nightingale, do not speak of the lark
Do not speak of the little wagtail
Who with his tail writes figures on the light.
I do not know a great deal about houses:
They have their own temper; that is all I know.
New at first, like babies
Who play in gardens with the tassels of the sun,
They do their embroideries with coloured shutters
And doors brilliantly shining on the screen of the day.
When the architect has finished, then they change,
They wrinkle up, they smile, or again grow obstinate
With those who stayed behind and with those who left,
With others who would return there if they could,
Or who have become lost now that this had happened,——
The world become a limitless inn for strangers.

I do not know a great deal about houses;
I remember their joy and their sorrow

Sometimes, when I stand still;
                              and also
At times, near the sea, in rooms stripped naked
With a single iron bedstead and nothing that is mine
Looking at the evening spider I call to mind
That such a one is getting ready to come, that they adorn him
In clothes of white and black with coloured jewels,
And around him is the slow speech of respected ladies,
With their grey hair and their dark lace;——
That he gets ready to come to say goodbye to me.
Or a woman deep-girdled, with glancing eyes,
Returning home from harbours of the south,
Smyrna, Rhodes, Syracuse, Alexandria,
From cities closed like shutters closed in the heat,
With perfume of golden fruit, and aromatic herbs,
That she is climbing the stairs without paying attention
To those who have gone to sleep underneath the stairs.

You find houses get obstinate easily, when you strip them naked.

II

The Lustful Elpenor

I saw him yesterday stop by the door,
Down from my window. It was round about
Seven o'clock and there was a woman with him.
He had the look of Elpenor just before
He fell and broke; and yet he was not drunk.
He was speaking very quickly, and the woman
Looked in an absent way towards the gramophones;
She stopped him occasionally to say a word or two
And then she would look away impatiently
To where they were frying fish. Like a cat looks.
He whispered with a fag-end in his lips:

'Listen again to this. I have seen by moonlight
Sometimes the statues leaning over like reeds
In the middle of living fruit,—the statues,
And the flame becomes a dewy oleander,
The flame that burns the man, I mean to say.'

'A trick of the light . . . the effect of the night shadows'

'The night perhaps: which opened, a blue pomegranate,
Dark breasts, filling you full of stars,
Cutting down time.

                   But all the same the statues
Sometimes do bend, and they deal out desire
Into two parts, like a peach shared, and the flame

[95]

Becomes a kiss on the limbs, a sobbing of breath
And then a cool leaf the wind carries away.
They bend, they become light with a human weight.
You cannot forget it.'

'The statues are in the museum.'

'No it is you they hunt. Why can't you see?
I mean the statues with their broken limbs
And faces from another time you have never
Seen and yet you know them.
                                        It is like
At the end of your youth you happen to be in love
With a woman who has kept her beauty. Holding
Her naked body in the noon, always
You fear the memory that surges up
To your embrace, you fear the kiss betraying you
To other beds which now are in time past,
And yet, for all that, there are ghosts might stalk there
Easily, so easily, and bring to life
Images to the mirror, bodies that were once,
And all the lust they had then.
                                        It is like
Coming back from a foreign land you chance to open
An old chest that for long has been locked up;
And there you find bits and pieces of the dresses
You wore in lovely times, in lighted revels
Of many colours, mirrored, which all fade,

And remains only the perfume of the absence
Of a young face.

             Oh it is true; the fragments
Are not the statues. You are yourself the remains.
They haunt you with their strange virginity
At home or office, at the big receptions
For honoured people, in your unconfessed
Terror of sleep. They speak of what you wish
Had never happened, or could happen years
After your death. Difficult, because——'

                     'The statues are in the museum.
Good-night.'

     'Because the statues are no more fragments.
We are. The Statues lightly bend. . . . Good night.'

At this they separated and he took
The upper road that leads towards the Bear.
And she went forward to the lighted beach
Where the wave is drowned in the roar of the radio:

The Radio

'Sails in the breath of the wind
That was all that the mind
Kept of the day; silence and scent of the pine
Easily they will cover the wound that is mine
The wound that they made when they left me behind
The sailor, the wagtail, the bullhead, the flycatcher too.

[97]

O woman insensitive, you
Hear of the death of the wind.

The golden barrel is done
And a rag is what was the sun,
A rag on the neck of a woman in middle age
Who coughs and who never stops coughing. What can assuage
Her grief for the summer that journeyed and left her behind,
For the gold on the shoulders and gold in the pit of the thighs?
O woman deprived of your eyes,
Hear me, the singer is blind.

Night falls, Shut the house fast.
Make flutes of the reeds of the past.
Open the window no more, however much they
Knock at the pane. They shout but have nothing to say.
Bring cyclamen, bring needles of pine and grasses,
Lilies out of the sand and anemones out of the sea.
O woman, mindless, hear me,
The water's funeral passes. . . .

—Athens, the situation rapidly
Deteriorates. The public are alarmed.
The Minister declared: No time is left. . . .
Bring cyclamen and bring the pine needles. . . .
And lilies from the sand . . . the pine needles. . . .
O woman. . . . There is an immense disparity.
The War——'

ARES DEALER IN SOULS

[98]

III

The Wreck of the 'Thrush'

'This wood which used to bring refreshment to my brow
In times when mid-day sun put fire into the veins,
In foreign hands will blossom. Take it. I give it to you.
Look, the wood is of a lemon tree. . . .'

                                I heard the voice
When staring into the sea I tried to distinguish
A ship which many years ago they had sunk there.
The ship's name was 'The Thrush', a small wreck, and the masts
Broken, groped to the bottom oblique, like tentacles,
Or memory of dreams, indicating the hull,
An indistinguishable mouth of some sea-creature, dead,
Quenched in the water. There was total calm around.

And little by little other voices in their turn
Followed in whisperings; they were thin and thirsty
And came from the other side of the sun, the dark side;
You would say they sought to drink blood, just a drop of it.
Familiar voices but I could not recognise them.
And then there came that old man's voice, this one I felt
Drop to the heart of the day
Calm, changeless, still:
'If you sentence me to drink poison, I thank you.
Your law shall be made my law. And where should I go
Running about in foreign lands, a rolling stone?
I choose death rather.
Which of us goes to the better fate God knows.'

[99]

Lands of sun, where you cannot face the sun.
Lands of man, where you cannot face the man.

As the years pass
So increase in number the judges who condemn you.
As the years pass and you speak with fewer voices,
You look with other eyes upon the sun.
You know that those who remained were cheating you;
Flesh's delirium, the lovely dance
That ends in nakedness.
As when, at night, turning into an empty highway
You suddenly see an animal's shining eyes
Which have already gone, so you feel your own eyes;
You stare at the sun, and then you are lost in the dark.
The doric chiton
Your fingers touched and it bent like the mountains
Is a marble image in light, but its head is in darkness.
And those who left the palaestra to take their bows
And shot the marathon runner full of the will to win;
And he saw the laps of the track sailing in blood
The world grow empty like the waning moon,
Victorious gardens withering away;
You see them in the sun, behind the sun.
And the boys who were doing diving from the bow-sprits
Go down like spindles, spinning round and round,
Bare bodies plunging into the black light,
With a coin between the teeth, still swimming on,
As the sun picks out with golden needlework

[100]

Sails, wet wood and colours of the deep sea;
Even now they go down obliquely
Down to the stones of the deep,
White shining jars.

Angelic and black light,
Laughter of waves on highways of the sea,
Laughter between the tears,
The old man in supplication looks on you
As he makes his way over invisible folds,
Light mirrored in his blood
From which sprang Eteokles and Polynikes.
Angelic and black day;
The brackish taste of woman that poisons the captive
Springs from the wave, fresh sprig with sea drops on it;
O sing, little Antigone, sing O sing. . . .
I do not speak of the past, I speak of love;
Crown your hair with thorns of the sun, dark girl.
The heart of the Scorpion has set,
The tyrant inside man has gone,
And all the daughters of the deep,
Nereids, Graiae
Run to the dazzle of the springs of light.
He who has never loved shall love, in the light.
                                        And you find yourself
In a great house with many windows open
Running from room to room, not knowing where first to look out.
Because the pines will go, and the mirrored mountains

And the chirping of birds.
The sea will empty, shattered glass, from North and South.
Your eyes will be emptied of the light of the day
As suddenly, of one accord, all the cicadas cease.

VII

FROM LOGBOOK III

———

"... Κύπρον οὗ μ'ἐθέσπισεν ..."
Euripides, Helen, 148.

Ayianapa I

And you see the light of the sun, just as the ancients used to say.
Yet I thought that I was seeing, all these years
Walking between the mountains and the sea
And meeting men full armed in perfect panoplies.
Strange, that I did not notice that all I saw was their voice.
It was the blood that made them speak, the ram
I slaughtered and was laying at their feet;
But that was not the light, not that red carpet.
Whatever they told me I had to feel with my hands,
As when they hide you, hunted, at night in a stable
Or as when you reach in the end a woman's flesh, deep-bosomed,
And the room is full and crowded with stifling odours;
Everything they told me was hide and silk.

Strange, I can see it here, the light of the sun, the gold net
Where things are quivering like the fishes
Which a great angel draws
Together with the nets of the fishermen.

'I Call You in the Goddess' Name...'

Oil upon the limbs
And perhaps a rancid smell
As here beside the oil mill
Of the little church
Or upon the coarsened pores
Of the still, unmoving stone.

Oil upon the hair and
A wreath of rope about it
And perhaps some other scents
Which we do not know about
Poor scents and rich scents
And little statues offering
Small breasts in their fingers.

Oil in the sun;
All the leaves were trembling
At the stranger's stopping there
And heavier between the knees
The weight of silence grew.
Down fell the coins;—'I call
You in the Goddess' name.'

Oil upon the shoulders
And on the twisting flanks
Sun-flecked legs in the grass,

And that wound struck in the sun
As they rang the vesper bell
As I spoke in the church yard
With a crippled man.

Three Mules

And the queen mounted on the wonderful mule called Margarita, which had belonged to her husband King Peter, and she sat upon the wonderful mule as women do; and she ordered her squire who was called Putsurello to bring her spurs with him. And she said to him: When I make a sign to you, turn my foot over so that I sit like a man and put on my spurs.

Chronicle of Makhairas

In Damascus one night of sleeplessness
There appeared to me the passing of Um Haram,
The very reverend kinswoman of the Prophet.
I heard the patter of hooves like silver dinars,
Then she, as though she were crossing hills of salt,
On the road to Larnaca, astride on her mule.
I was there waiting among the cool branches,
Biting the fruit of myrtle;
And my eyes were stung by a whiteness,
Perhaps the salt, perhaps her ghost. And then
A whisper in the bushes:
                              'Here it was
That my beast slipped. And this the stone
That broke my lily neck,
And I gave up my soul victorious.
I was full of the will of God,
And that was too much weight for a beast to bear.
Do not forget this, and do not wrong the mule.'

She spoke and vanished. Yet even now
That mule of hers is grazing in my brain,

As is that other one, whose heart stopped still
When they lifted from her back the weight of coffins,
The two brothers, unjustly done to death
By the public hangman there on Koutsoventi.
But the greatest one of them all, how shall I tell of her?
In the country where those who lived below the castellos
Have been forgotten like last year's upturned earth,
She still goes sailing on the wings of fame,
The glorious animal of Queen Eleanor.
Against her belly those eperons of gold,
On her saddle those insatiable loins,
In her amble tottering those breasts
Bursting, like pomegranates, with murder.
And when Neapolitans, Genoese and Lombards
Brought to the royal table on a silver tray
The shirt all bloody of the murdered King
And made away with his pitiable brother,
I can imagine how she neighed that night,——
Something beyond the impassivity of her race,——
Like the howling of a dog,
Doubly caparisoned, golden-rumped, in the stable,
Margarita, that mule.

Salamis in Cyprus

. . . and Salamis, the mother-city of which is the cause of our present woes.

Aeschylus, The Persians

At times the sun of mid-day, at times the handfuls of light rain
And the beach full of fragments of ancient sherds.
The columns, unimportant. There is only Saint Epiphanios
Dimly radiant of that absorbed might of the golden Empire.
The flesh and blood of the young, loved and loving, have passed here;
Those beating hearts, rose-pink of shells, the light feet
Fearlessly skimming the water,
And arms opened for the joining of desire.
The Lord upon many waters,
Here upon this place of passing.

Then I heard footsteps upon the pebbles
I saw no faces. They had gone when I turned my head.
Still that voice heavy upon me like the treading of cattle
Stayed in the pulses of the sky and in the sea's roll
Over upon the shingle again and again:

'The earth has no handles
For them to lift it on their shoulders and take it away.
They are not able, however thirsty,
To sweeten the salt sea with half a cup-full of water.
And those bodies
Created from a land unknown to them
Have their own souls.

Now they assemble tools to change these souls.
It will not be possible. They will only undo them,
If souls can be undone.
It does not take long for the corn to ripen
No time is needed
For the yeast of bitterness to rise,
No time is needed
For evil to raise its head,
And the sick mind drained empty,
No time is needed
For the filling of this with madness.
There is an island.'

Friends of the other war,
On this desolate and cloudy beach
I call you to mind, as the day is turning,——
Who fell in the fighting, who fell long after the battle,
Who saw the dawn rising through the mist of death,
Or, in wild solitude below the stars,
Felt upon their skin the great dark eyes
Of absolute disaster;
And, once again, those who prayed
When the ships were being sawn by the burning steel:
'O Lord, help us to keep in mind
How this murder came about;
Greed, dishonesty, selfishness,
The drying up of love.
Lord help us to root out these things.'

[111]

—Now, among these pebbles, it is better to forget;
It does no good to speak.
What the powerful have determined, who can change it?
And who can make himself heard?
Each has his dreams apart; unknown to him the nightmares
That vex the others' sleep.
—True. But the messenger is on his way
And, however long his journey, he will bring
To those who tried to put fetters on the Hellespont
The fearful message that came from Salamis.

Voice of the Lord upon the waters.
There is an island.

November, 1953

Memory I

'And there was no more sea'

And I with my hands holding nothing but a reed;
The night was desolate, the moon was on the wane
And the earth smelling of the last shower of rain.
I whispered: memory, wherever you touch it, gives pain,
There is little sky and there is no more sea,
They cart off what they kill by day and dispose of it behind the ridge.
My fingers were playing with this pipe absentmindedly.
I wished an old shepherd good evening and he gave it to me.
The others have done away with every greeting;
They wake, they shave, they start the day's work of killing,
Like pruning or surgery, with method and with no feeling;
Pain is a corpse like Patroclus and nobody makes a mistake.

I thought of playing a tune, and then I was ashamed of the other world
The one that sees me from beyond the night from within my light
Which is woven from living bodies, from naked hearts,
And the love which belongs also to those Dread Goddesses
Just as to man and to stone, to the waters and to the grasses,
And to the animal staring in death's eyes as death comes to take it.

So I went up the dark path. I turned in
At my garden gate. I dug and buried the reed.
And again I whispered: one dawn will come the Resurrection,
As trees shine in the spring, so will gleam the dew of that morning,
Once more the sea, and again Aphrodite shaken out from the wave's foam;
We are the seed that dies. And I went into my empty home.

[113]

Helen

TEUCER: . . . *towards sea surrounded Cyprus, where Apollo said*
I was to settle down and call my city's name
Salamis, in memory of my old island home. . . .

HELEN: *I never went to Troy. Only a phantom went. . . .*

MESSENGER: *What's this? Then did we toil in vain there simply for a cloud?*

Euripides, Helen

'The nightingales will never let you go to sleep at Platres.'

Shy nightingale, in the shuddering breath of the leaves,
Giver of dewy music, the dew of the forest,
To bodies parted each from each, to the souls
Of those who know that they will not come back again.
Blind voice, in the darkened memory turning over
Footsteps, gestures of hands, I'd not dare say kisses,
And the bitter heave of the heart, the heart of a slave grown savage.

'The nightingales will never let you go to sleep at Platres.'

Platres, what is it? Who is it knows this island?
I have lived my life hearing names heard for the first time;
New places and new madnesses
Whether of men or gods.
                              My own fate which wavers
Between the final sword of an Ajax
And another Salamis
Has brought me to this shore; here the moon
Has risen from the sea like Aphrodite,

Has blotted out the Archer, and now she goes,
To the Heart of the Scorpion, changing everything.
O truth, where are you?
I also was an archer in the war;
My fate that of a man who missed the mark.

Melodious nightingale,
On such a night as this the Spartan slave girls
Heard you on Proteus's beach and lifted their lament.
And among them there was—who could have thought it?—Helen!
She, our pursuit for years beside Scamander.
She was there, at the desert's edge. I touched her. She spoke to me.
'It is not true, it is not true', she cried.
'I never went aboard that coloured ship;
I never trod the ground of manly Troy.'

Deep-girdled, the sun in her hair, with that way of standing,
The print of shadows and the print of smiles
On shoulders, thighs and knees,
The lively skin, the eyes and the great eyelids,
She was there, on the banks of a Delta.
                              And at Troy?
Nothing. At Troy a phantom.
So the gods willed it.
And Paris lay with a shadow as though it were solid flesh:
And we were slaughtered for Helen ten long years.

Great pain had fallen on Greece.
So many bodies thrown

To jaws of the sea, to jaws of the earth;
So many souls
Given up to the mill-stones to be crushed like corn.
And the muddy beds of the rivers sweated with blood
For a wavering linen garment, a thing of air,
For a butterfly's jerk, for a swan's down, for a Helen.
And my brother?
                    O nightingale, nightingale,
What is god? What is not god? What is in-between?

'The nightingales will never let you go to sleep at Platres!'

Tearful bird,
                    at sea-kissed Cyprus,
Ordained for me to remind me of my country,
I moored alone and brought this fairy story,
If it is true that it is a fairy story,
If it is true that man will not set in motion once more
The old deceit of the gods;
                              if it is true
That after many years some other Teucer,
Some Ajax, maybe, or Priam or Hecuba,
Or someone quite unknown, nameless, yet one who saw
The corpses crown the banks of a Scamander,
Were not so fated as this—fated to hear
The steps of messengers, who come to tell him
That so much suffering, so much of life
Fell into the abyss
For the sake of an empty garment, for a Helen.

[116]

Euripides the Athenian

He lived and grew old between the burning of Troy
And the hard labour in Sicilian quarries.

He was fond of rocky caves along the beach;
Liked pictures of the sea;
The veins of man he saw as it were a net
Made by the Gods for trapping us like beasts.
This net he tried to pierce.
He was difficult in every way. His friends were few.
The time arrived and he was torn to pieces by dogs.

Pentheus

Asleep he was filled with dreams of fruits and leaves;
Awake he was not permitted to pick one berry.
Sleep and wakefulness shared out his limbs to the Bacchae.

Memory II

Ephesus

As he spoke he was sitting on a piece of marble
That appeared to be some part of an ancient gateway;
To the right stretched out the endless empty plain,
To the left came down from the mountain the final shadows.
'The poem is everywhere. Your voice sometimes
Rises, emerges at its side, like the dolphin
That for a while accompanies the journey
Of some swift golden schooner in the sun
And then is lost again. The poem is everywhere
Like those wings of the wind within the wind
That touched just for one moment the seagull's wings.
Our life itself, yet different, just as when
Woman's nakedness is revealed and her face changes
And yet is the same face. Those who have loved
Know this. The world, in the light of other people,
Withers away. But this you must remember:
Hades and Dionysus are the same.'
He spoke these words and then he took the highway
That leads to the ancient harbour over there,
All overgrown with rushes. The twilight
Was, you might say, for the death of an animal,
So naked was it.
    I can still remember;
He was on his way to the Ionian headlands,
To empty shells of theatres where now

[118]

Only the lizard crawls on the dry stones,
And I asked him 'Will they ever be full again?'
And he replied 'Perhaps, at the hour of death.'
And he rushed into the orchestra, yelling out,
'O let me listen to my brother's voice!'
And the silence stood around us hard as rock,
Making no trace upon the glass of the blue.

Engomi

The plain was wide and level; in the distance you could see
Hands turn in the motion of digging.
In the sky the clouds were ringlets; here and there
A trumpet of gold and rose: the approaching dusk.
In the scanty grass and among the thorns there roamed
Thin breaths that follow the rain; it must have been raining
Over there at the edge of the hills that now took on colour.

And I went forward to the people who were working,
Women and men with picks working in ditches.
It was an ancient city; walls, streets and houses there stood out,
Fossilised muscles of Cyclopean giants,
Spent power in its anatomy, under the eye of
Archaeologist, anaesthetist or surgeon.
Phantoms and fabrics, luxury and lips dissolved,
And the curtains of suffering drawn right back
Revealing the naked, indifferent tomb.

And I looked up towards the people who were working,
The straining shoulders, the arms striking down
A heavy beat, a tattoo on this world of the dead,
As if through the ruins the wheel of fate was rolling.

Suddenly I was walking and not walking.
I looked at the flying birds: they had turned to stone.
I looked at the shining sky: there was amazement in the air

I looked at the struggling bodies: they stood still.
And in their midst was a face ascending into the light.
Over the neck the black hair flowed, the eyebrows
Had the beat of a swallow's wing, the nostrils
Curved back over the lips, and now the body
Was rising out of the labour, naked, with the unripe breasts
Of a virgin, Leader of Ways;
A dancing but no movement.

And I turned my eyes down to look about me.
I saw girls kneading bread—and their hands not touching the dough,
Women spinning—and the spindles did not turn,
Sheep at the drinking trough—and the sheeps' tongues stuck still
Over the green waters that seemed to be sunk in sleep;
And the shepherd stayed with his crook uplifted into the air.
And I looked again at that ascending body;
Multitudes had assembled together, a swarm of ants,
And were striking her with spears and not hurting her.
And now as I saw her belly shine out like the moon,
This was my belief, that the sky was the womb which bore her
And which now was taking her back, mother and babe.
Still her feet remained. The feet were of marble.
They vanished: an Assumption.
                    The world
Was becoming again what it was: our own,
The world of time and of earth.
                    Perfumes of terebinth
Began to move and stir along the old slopes of memory,

Breasts on a couch of leaves, moistness of lips,
And everything at once dried up in the stretch of the plain
In the wilderness of the stones, in the power eaten away,
In the empty land with its scanty grass and the thorns
Where slithered the body of a snake uncaring,
Where they spend much time in dying.

NOTES

Notes

1. *Biographical*

George Seferis is the pen name of George Seferiades who was born in Smyrna on the 29th February, 1900. His family moved to Athens in 1914. From 1918 to 1924 he studied in Paris and in 1926 joined the Greek Diplomatic Service. His first appointment abroad was to London in 1931. Subsequently he held other diplomatic posts, including that of Consul in Koritsa (Albania). At the time of the German invasion of Greece he followed the Free Greek Government and served in Crete, South Africa, Egypt, Palestine, London and Italy. In 1944, at the time of the liberation, he returned to Athens and since 1948 has again served abroad in Turkey, Lebanon, Syria, Jordan and Iraq. For the last three years he has been Ambassador in London. He is married.

2. *Bibliographical*

The following are the titles and dates of publications by George Seferis: 'Turning Point' (*Στροφή*) Athens, 1931; 'The Cistern', Athens, 1932; 'Mythistorema', Athens, 1935; 'T. S. Eliot (Introduction and Translations)', Athens, 1936; 'A dialogue on Poetry', Athens, 1939; 'Log Book I', Athens, 1940; 'Exercise Book' Athens, 1940; 'Poems I', Athens, 1940; 'Essays', Cairo, 1944; 'Log Book II' (printed in facsimile of author's hand writing) Alexandria, 1944 and Icaros, Athens, 1945; 'Erotokritos' (an essay) Athens, 1946; 'The "Thrush"', Icaros, Athens, 1947; 'Collected Poems 1924-1946', Icaros, Athens, 1950; 'Three days at the Monasteries of Cappadocia', French Institute, Athens, 1953; 'Sidney Keyes: "The Wilderness"' (a translation) Athens, 1954; 'Log Book III' (under the title '. . . *Κύπρον οὗ μ'ἐθέσπισεν* . . .'), Icaros, Athens, 1955.

3. *Notes on the Text*

p. 9   'Mythistorema': Of the use of this compound word Seferis writes: 'This title was chosen for its two components: *Myth*, because I have obviously used a certain mythology; and *History*, because I tried to convey in a certain sequence a state of mind as independent from mine as that of characters in a novel.' It should be added that the word is commonly used in Greek to mean a novel.

p. 12 'The fingers on the rim, as the poet says': cf. Dionysios Solomos, *The Woman of Zante:*
'And the just according to the Holy Scripture, how many are they? And thinking of this, my eyes played upon my hands that were resting on the rim. And wanting to count on my fingers the just, I lifted from the rim my left hand, and looking at the fingers of my right hand, I said: Would those be too many?'

p. 12 'Remember the baths. . . .' Aeschylus, *Choephoroi*, 491.

p. 13 'And for the soul if it is to know itself it is into a soul that it must look': Plato, *Alcibiades*, 133c.

p. 26 'The name—Orestes', Sophocles, *Electra* 694.

p. 31 'Let them turn toward Erebus. . . .' cf. Homer, *Odyssey*, X, 528.

p. 50 'I-ow! I-ow! . . . Pew-pax'. Aeschylus, *Eumenides*, 143.

p. 52 'The Aegean flower with corpses'. Aeschylus, *Agamemnon*, 659.

p. 67 'And our women working . . . quarries'. cf. *Iliad* VI, 457 and Thucydides VI, 87.

p. 71 ''Ασίνην τε'=And Asine. Pronounced: Asinen té

p. 80 'At Psara on the blackened slope'. cf. Dionysios Solomos' epigram:
'At Psara on the blackened slope
Glory walks alone.
Her mind is bent on gallant lads;
On her hair she wears a wreathe
Twined from the few grasses
That still remained upon the ravaged earth.'

p. 90 'Sorrow-recalling pain'. Aeschylus, *Agamemnon*, 179.

p. 98 'Ares dealer in souls'. cf. Aeschylus, *Agamemnon*, 438.

p. 99 'If you sentence me to drink poison. . . .' cf. Plato, the end of the *Apology*.

p. 101 'The old man in supplication. . . .' Sophocles, cf. *Oedipus Colone us* 1679 sq.

p. 106 'I call you in the Goddess' name'. cf. Herodotus, I, 199: 'There is one custom amongst these people (the Babylonians) which is wholly shameful: every woman who is a native of the country must once in her life go and sit in the temple of Aphrodite and there give herself to a strange man. . . . Most sit in the precinct of the temple with a band of plaited string

[126]

round their heads . . . Once a woman has taken her seat she is not allowed to go home until a man has thrown a silver coin into her lap and taken her outside to lie with her. As he throws the coin, the man has to say 'In the name of the goddess Mylitta'—that being the Assyrian name for Aphrodite. . . . There is a custom similar to this in parts of Cyprus'.

p. 111 '. . . those who prayed when the ships. . . .' On this line Seferis writes: 'In some South African newspaper I had read (September 1941) the prayer which Lord Hugh Beresford, R.N., had composed for his ship: "O God our loving Father. . . . Help us to keep in mind the real causes of war: dishonesty, greed, selfishness, and lack of love, and to drive them out of this ship, so that she may be a pattern of the new world for which we are fighting. . . ." He fell in the battle of Crete'.

R. W.